PAN DULCE
1 2 3

Dedicated to Helena, an explorer of
wonder and boundless adventures.
May your curiosity and passion
light up countless worlds.

© 2023 Monarch Libros. All rights reserved.

First paperback edition November 2023

Illustrated by Vanessa Suarez

ISBN 979-8-9893701-0-8 (Paperback)
ISBN 979-8-9893701-1-5 (ebook)
ISBN 979-8-9893701-3-9 (Hardcover)

Library of Congress Control Number: 2023920896

Published by Monarch Libros
www.monarchlibros.com

Amelia and her family are super excited for a special day at their favorite bakery, the Panaderia! They can't wait to gobble up the yummy pan dulce. Amelia loves numbers and wants to count all the yummy pan dulce! Let's count together with her!

¡Amelia y su familia están súper emocionados porque van a visitar su lugar favorito: ¡la Panadería! Sienten que ya no pueden esperar más para devorar todo el delicioso pan dulce posible. ¡Amelia ama los números y quiere contar todo el delicioso pan dulce! ¡Contemos juntos con ella!

$0.79
galletas grageas

$0.69
galletas sonrisas

$0.89
puerquitos

one uno

un puerquito

two dos

dos conchas

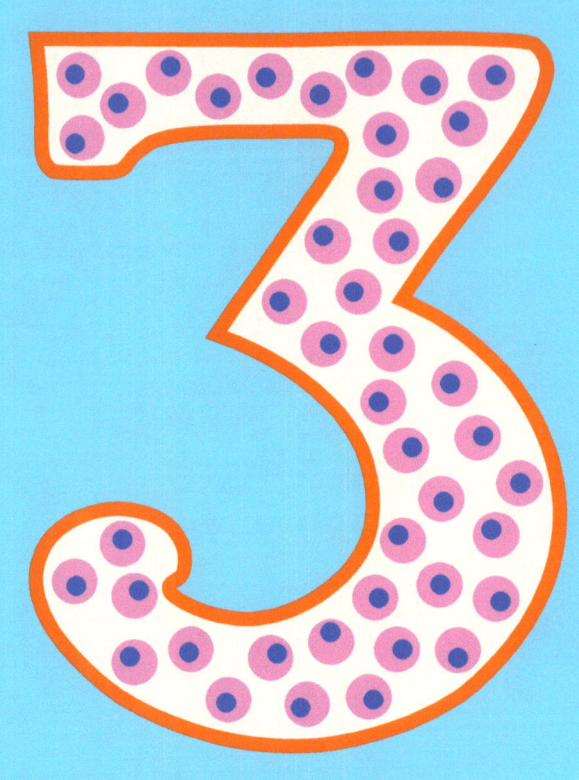

three tres

tres cuernitos

four cuatro

cuatro orejitas

five cinco

cinco galletas sonrisas

six seis

seis polvorones tricolor

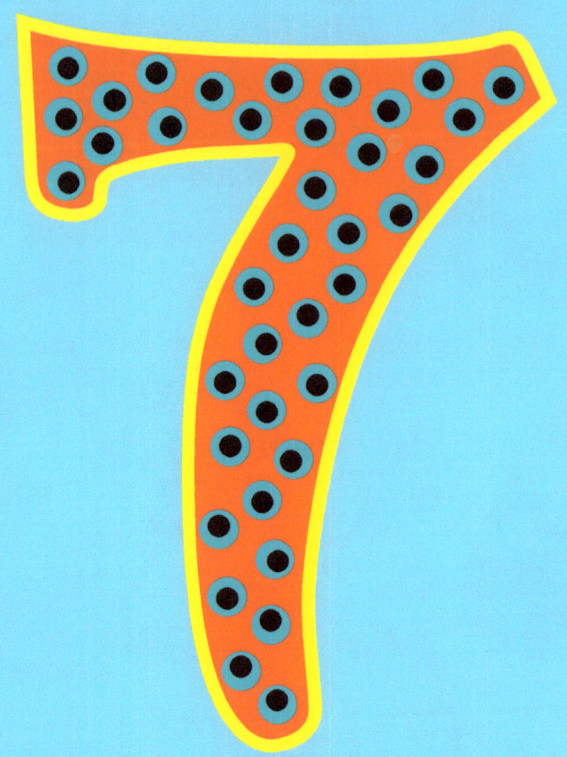

seven siete

siete ratones de chocolate

8

eight **ocho**

ocho churros

nine nueve

nueve niños envueltos

ten **diez**

diez galletas de gragea

PAN DULCE

Puerquito

Concha

Cuernito

Orejita

Galleta Sonrisa

Polvorone Tricolor

Raton de Chocolate

Churro

Niño Envuelto

Galleta de Gragea